MW00641361

The Spiritual Resilience Handbook

A faith-based, research-informed, practical approach

Connie Fourré

ISBN 978-1-7360072-0-4

Table of Contents

Chapter 1: Introduction

W e live in turbulent times. Economic and political turmoil, a deadly virus, and the "normal" wear and tear of life can be overwhelming. There's ample cause for fear and sadness, but the anxiety and resentment we sometimes feel only make things worse.

Jesus knew that. In times as painful and uncertain as our own he told us not to worry, to be people of gratitude, hope and compassion. He encouraged us to be *spiritually resilient*: to keep a positive spirit and a sense of purpose and meaning even when the sky turns dark.

Some people come by these qualities naturally. Most of us wander off into the weeds if we're not paying attention. Fast-paced lives, heartbreaking news headlines, and our own personal difficulties challenge our ability to stay resilient and on track.

So how do we get there? How can we close the gap between where we are and where God calls us to be? How do we protect ourselves from the eroding power of anxiety and resentment? How can we open ourselves to grace with as much skill as we can muster? All too often our white-knuckled attempts to "be better" fall short.

This is a faith-based, research-informed approach to developing practical habits that are shown to improve wellbeing.

This book blends current scientific research on the human brain with ancient spiritual wisdom about the world and our place in it. This is a faith-based, research-informed approach to developing practical habits that have been shown to improve wellbeing, reduce anxiety and depression and–with God's grace–help us become closer to the persons we were created to be. While this method is adaptable to a wide range of perspectives on faith, these pages will feel most comfortable to people who believe in or are searching for God or a Higher Power.

Throughout history humans have divided ourselves along religious lines. We tend to quickly pigeonhole one another based on our theology or lack thereof. Though our differences are real and important, spiritual resilience work is more like a wellness program than a religion class. I write from my own Christian background, but this approach is adaptable to other faith traditions as well as to a secular perspective. I invite you to translate these pages into your own spiritual framework, taking what's useful and leaving the rest.

Introduction

WHAT IS SPIRITUAL RESILIENCE?

Spiritual resilience is *the ability to maintain a sturdy positive spirit and a clear sense of purpose and meaning even in the face of suffering.*

We intuitively recognize this quality when we see it. Spiritually resilient people are generally calm, hopeful and kind. We're drawn to them and somehow feel better when we're in their presence. They have a strength that radiates from within and a dedication to others' welfare. They are willing to engage with their own and others' suffering.

More often than most, spiritually resilient people experience these positive emotions:
- Gratitude
- Hope
- Compassion
- Awe
- Serenity
- Joy
- Inspiration
- Love

You'll notice these emotions feel good while at the same time moving us beyond our own egos to connect with other people and a reality greater than ourselves. Research shows these emotions have the power to heal us physically and emotionally and increase our capacity to reach out and change the world for the better.

This book will examine how we can develop concrete, practical habits that deepen the presence of these emotions in our lives. This work is likely to strengthen the other two aspects of spiritual resilience: our sense of purpose and meaning and our ability to deal constructively with our own and others' pain. However, our primary focus is on enhancing our spiritual/ emotional wellbeing. We will reserve more focused attention on the other two aspects of resilience for another book.

HOW THIS WORKS

Spiritual practices are *things we do on a regular basis to help bring us back to center.* They involve our whole selves –body, mind and spirit–rather than just our intellects. This book will introduce you to, or remind you of, six traditional spiritual practices:
* Gratitude
* Blessing
* Surrender/letting go
* Music
* One-liners
* Service

Research shows these spiritual habits substantially increase wellbeing while reducing anxiety, resentment and depression. While it's not possible to guarantee specific results for any one individual, these practices have been around for centuries because they help. Incorporating what science now teaches us about the mind/body/spirit connection makes them even more transformative. Done alone or with others, they help us thrive and make the world a better place.

THE POWER IS IN THE DOING

More than once when browsing in a boutique shop I've seen a post, "Sure, you could make it yourself. But *will* you?" Knowing how to do something isn't enough. Simply understanding spiritual emotions and practices doesn't change anything, any more than buying an exercise bike makes us fit. Actually *engaging* in spiritual practices has a positive impact on our nervous systems and opens us up to the grace of God we so often pass by. Lasting change comes hard. My prayer is that these pages will support you in bringing these habits to life.

NUTS AND BOLTS

Unless you live in a monastery, you are not likely to use all of these practices every day. I would encourage you to read the chapters one at a time and give yourself at least a week with each one to try out what you learn. This will give you a chance to see for yourself if the recommendations help. The goal is to become familiar enough with the practices so you can effectively integrate them into your life.

You'll find action recommendations at the end of each chapter. Research shows we are more likely to follow through on a new plan for action when we:

1) Make a specific commitment and
2) Anticipate obstacles and plan around them

There is space at the end of each chapter for you to write down your intentions and your plan to counter obstacles. I invite you to do both.

WE'RE STRONGER TOGETHER

If possible, I encourage you to find a buddy or a small group to begin this adventure together. Partners not only help us stay accountable; they also share stories and encouragement along the way. I have been part of a spiritual accountability group for more than thirty years, and it has helped me stay anchored through storms and calm. There is a kind of connection that happens in spiritual sharing that is precious and all too rare. Our most powerful conversations are not about theory. They happen when we share how we are being shaped by what we believe and practice. I hope you can find at least one person to walk this path with you.

ACTION PLAN

Let's say for the sake of argument that incorporating these spiritual practices into your life would accomplish most, if not all, of the following:

- Increase your experience of at least some of the spiritual emotions listed
- Decrease your experience of anxiety and/or depression, if you have them
- Offer you more meaningful and enjoyable connections with others
- Give you a language you can use with people who see religion and spirituality differently than you do
- Increase your ability to act compassionately

If that were true, how much time would you be willing to commit to the experiment over the next two months? (I'd recommend around 30 minutes per week with the chapter, and 10-15 minutes per day, five or so days a week for the practices.)

I commit myself to:

What obstacles do you expect will get in the way? What can you do to manage them?

Chapter 2: Gratitude

Y ou should be grateful!

We've all heard those words, most often when we weren't in the mood to listen. We've scolded ourselves for not being grateful–also, most likely, when gratitude wasn't coming easily.

Yet gratitude is one of the most powerful tools in our arsenal for building spiritual resilience. Research shows gratitude actually holds the power to nudge us away from depression and anxiety and toward greater peace with ourselves and our world.

SO WHAT EXACTLY *IS* GRATITUDE?

Gratitude is not the same as appreciation, although appreciation is a good place to start. When we appreciate something or someone, we stop to notice, to pay attention. We take the opportunity to register and savor the moment.

Appreciation takes the time to enjoy the good. Gratitude looks further to the *source* of the goodness. When I appreciate a plate of fajitas, I take a serious look at it, I smell the delicious aroma, I pay attention to what's on my fork and in my mouth without being overly distracted by what's going on in the room. I appreciate the meal but I'm not considering how the meal got to my plate.

When I'm grateful I also acknowledge the cook's skill and the time invested in preparing the meal. I can grow my circle of gratitude to include the farmers who raised and harvested the ingredients and the truckers who transported them to my grocery store. If I dig even deeper I can expand my scope to include the planet that sustains my life and ultimately the One who created it all.

The online Oxford Dictionary goes one step further, defining gratitude as thankfulness and "a readiness to show appreciation for and to return kindness." Gratitude can turn a humble plate of fajitas into a moment of spiritual re-centering.

Simply telling ourselves or our children to be grateful doesn't necessarily make much difference. However, consciously, specifically and thoughtfully shifting our attention toward the blessings in our lives can.

Our gratitude can extend to painful as well as pleasurable moments. I used to ask my high school students to list fifty things they were grateful for. I knew a shorter assignment would likely generate a whole lot of clichés, but as the students stretched to fill those last twenty slots, their lists became much more interesting. I will never forget one student's entry. She'd been injured as an infant while in the care of a negligent babysitter, and her beautiful face bore a noticeable scar even after several surgeries. On her list, without any explanation, was, "My scar." Her ability to find the bittersweet blessing in her experience had brought her wisdom at a very young age.

A GRATITUDE PRACTICE

Gratitude is both an emotion and a spiritual practice. A spiritual practice is *a concrete action we engage in on a regular basis in order to bring ourselves back to what's real.* Spiritual practices are intentional behaviors, some of which are obvious to others and some that happen only within our minds and hearts. Regularly *practicing* gratitude over time helps us *be* grateful people.

There are many ways to develop a regular gratitude practice. A few examples:

1) Like my students, you could make a list of 50 things you're grateful for and try to review it frequently.

2) An alternative is to choose a time or event that happens regularly in your day, such as a meal, waking up in the morning, commuting, etc. Commit to thanking God in that moment for five people or things in your life.

3) Make a decision to count your blessings when you're tempted to ruminate about the latest news story.

4) Write a letter of gratitude to a person who has helped you along the way. If possible, deliver it, whether in person, by snail mail or email, or over the phone.

5) Keep a gratitude journal. I recently attended a funeral where excerpts from my dear friend's gratitude journal were read. It was a touching reminder of who she was and an example of the legacy she left to her children, grandchildren and friends.

6) Draw gratitude pictures, and invite the children–or the adult artists–in your life to do the same. Post them around your home, or share them on social media.

7) Have a designated gratitude jar or bowl, with a pen or markers and slips of paper nearby. Jot down gratitude moments as you think of them. If you live with other people, pull a few out and read them at mealtime.

A spiritual practice is a concrete action
we engage in on a regular basis
in order to bring ourselves back to what's real.

If these practices seem obvious and simple it's because they are. Change happens when we:

1) Actually do them regularly and
2) Do them mindfully, being truly present to the moment.

Here's where a piece of neuroscience comes in. Simply listing things intellectually activates only a small part of your brain and has virtually no impact on the rest of your body. We experience gratitude more deeply, and benefit more fully, if we engage our emotions in this practice. To do so, take time to really be present to each item on your list. Take a deep breath as you recall a person's face or the brilliant colors of a sunset. Consciously enlist your senses in your moment of gratitude. Focus long enough that the gratitude has a chance to actually register on a feeling level. This engages the emotional part of your brain, which then activates the rest of your nervous system. We store memories more vividly and securely under the influence of emotion.

Some days this will "work" and some days it won't, but our intention matters. There's a ton of research out there saying a gratitude practice can make you happier. You can check it out quickly by googling "gratitude benefits." If you prefer a more academic, scientific approach, search on Google Scholar. (https://scholar.google.com)

You can verify the scientific research on a small scale in your own life by noticing how you feel before and after a moment of gratitude. See if in fact those deliberate gratitude pauses give a lift to your day.

This week, look over the list and commit yourself to engage in one or two gratitude practices. Pick a "target frequency"–say four or five times a week–and give it your best shot for a couple of weeks. Ideally, tell at least one other person about your commitment, and then check in with them. Or encourage them to join you and share your experiences together. At the end of a week or two, look back and notice if your gratitude moments, taken as a whole, have made a difference.

ACTION PLAN

The gratitude practices I choose for this week are:

1)

2)

I commit to do practice 1 _____ *times this week.*

I commit to do practice 2 _____ *times this week.*

I will share this practice with:

No Pain No Gain

Chapter 3: No Pain No Gain...Really??

I n one way or another we begin teaching our children to ignore their bodies at a very young age. We expect them to sit silent and still in their school desks for hours every day, letting them outside briefly to laugh, jump and run around. We encourage our young athletes to play through their pain to the point where teenagers having knee and shoulder surgery seems normal to us. Many adults spend our working days hunched over computer keyboards or outside in extreme temperatures or engaged in countless damaging repetitive motions in a factory or checkout counter.

We learn to tune out the "Take a break!" messages our bodies send us because we are so intent on tasks, but our productivity comes at a price. Our bodies respond with inflamed tendons, acid reflux, insomnia and reduced resistance to disease. Their protests don't go away just because we refuse to pay attention. Stiff shoulders and tight guts continue to send messages to our brains about the safety or peril in any given moment.

We all know that stress can skew our thinking processes. Few of us realize just how many of our everyday choices are impacted by our unconscious derailed warning systems. Becoming more aware of what's happening in our bodies can help us make better decisions and lean into positive spiritual emotions like compassion, hope, joy and serenity.

INTRODUCING BODY AWARENESS

A first step toward healing the body/spirit disconnect is to deepen our awareness of our bodies. Bringing physical sensations into consciousness helps us listen to our body's wisdom, ("Get up and walk around for five minutes") and pay less attention to its false alarms, ("If I have to get up and speak in front of this group I'm going to die on the spot.")

Take a moment to consider precisely *where* you feel your stress: Is it in your gut? shoulders? forehead? back of neck? lower back? somewhere else? We each have our own unique responses.

When you feel happy, where does that emotion register in your body? Is it a warm feeling that spreads across your chest? Do your shoulders drop just a bit? Does your face relax into a smile? Does your breathing move from your chest to your diaphragm? What happens to you physically if you catch a glimpse of a night sky or a small child laughing? Take a few minutes to remember.

Anger and happiness are names and meanings we give to a constellation of sensations in our bodies. For example, when we perceive a threat our muscles tighten, our breath gets shallow, our hearts race–and we call that sensation fear. When we share a loving smile with someone our muscles relax, a sense of warmth permeates our bodies, and we call that reaction joy. Becoming more aware of the physical sensations underlying our emotions gives us a deeper awareness about ourselves. It increases our capacity to *respond* thoughtfully rather than simply *reacting* to the emotions coursing above or below our level of awareness.

> *A first step toward healing*
> *the body/spirit disconnect*
> *is to deepen our awareness of our bodies.*

THE METHOD

As an example, let's revisit your gratitude practice.

1) Begin by doing a self-inventory right now. What is your body sensing, and what emotion-name would you use to label it?
Descriptors for body sensations are words like *relaxed, tense, sore, warm, cold, tingly, heavy, etc.*
Names for emotions are *happy, tired, stressed, bored, sad, excited, etc.*
If you like, rate the intensity of what you're experiencing on a scale from 1 to 10.

2) Take a couple of deep breaths and settle into your chair or bed or wherever you find yourself. Place yourself

consciously in God's presence. Take another moment to notice your breathing. Then call to mind someone or something you are truly grateful for.

Let's say it's your favorite aunt. Take a minute to remember what her face looks like, how her voice sounds, how she dresses. Remember a special moment you had with her. How did you feel physically in that moment? Emotionally? How do you feel now as you recall it? (If she is somehow absent from you now, your current emotion may be sadness.) Thank God for her presence in your life. Stay with this for a bit, as best you can. If your thoughts race away, gently call them back.

3) Now check back in with your body and see if your physical sensations have changed. Are your muscles more relaxed? Your face softened? Do you have a different sensation in your chest or gut? Is there something else you notice? Try your 1-10 rating again and see if there's a difference. Which state do you prefer? Which helps you be your best self?

THE LIMITS OF EFFORT

You may or may not have been able to fully enter into this exercise today. That's normal. You are beginning to consciously train your body/brain, which is a lot like trying to train a two-month-old puppy.

Or a cat.

The work takes practice, and there is no straight path from Point A to Point B. Few of us will totally "get there" in this life.

Our bodies aren't machines and we can only influence, not control our emotional responses. We can manage ourselves only to a point and, as we seem to need to be reminded, we can't manipulate God at all. What we *can* do is create circumstances and practices that allow more space for our spirits to thrive.

We are created body/spirits, and our bodies have a significant impact on how we think and behave. Consciously asking God's help, relying on grace, and working *with* our bodies rather than ignoring them, can move us toward a more spiritually resilient response to the challenges and joys of our lives today.

A WORD ABOUT TRAUMA

Trauma needs to be considered in our individual responses to some of these exercises. Tuning out emotions and conscious connection with the body is a survival strategy for many who have experienced deep grief and trauma.

If you are now or have in the past carried a great deal of emotional pain, please be careful about re-engaging body awareness. This work asks us to be cautious and brave at the same time. Strategies that are helpful when we're ready can be risky when we're not. Please listen to your own inner wisdom, and terminate a practice and access professional help if you need to.

ACTION PLAN

My commitment to self-care around trauma (if needed)

I will consciously focus awareness on my body's sensations
_____ *times this week.* Jot down a place/time when that
will happen, if that would be helpful for you. (Ex: before
falling asleep, before a tense meeting, etc.)

Followup:

I became more aware that:

I was/n't more able to respond effectively:

Chapter 4: Asking Blessing

I always thought Mr. Rogers was fine. A little awkward, perhaps, but okay. His neighborhood wasn't as entertaining and smart as New York's *Sesame Street*, but I knew he tackled some tough topics and that my five children liked him. Once they grew up I pretty much forgot about him.

Until now. With so many others I was humbled by the documentary *Won't You Be My Neighbor?* and by Tom Hanks' portrayal of Mr. Rogers in *A Beautiful Day in the Neighborhood*. Fred Roger's quiet strength, courage and persistent kindness are especially compelling against the backdrop of our anxious and contentious era.

I was particularly touched as I watched the scene in *Beautiful Day* when Mr. Rogers lowers himself into a pool, adjusts his goggles, and sets out on his daily swim. With each stroke he remembers the name of a person he has promised to pray for, a list that's impressively long. I believe this habit was both an expression of and a support for his remarkable spirit.

Many of us grew up with the nightly ritual of asking, "God bless Mommy and Daddy and..." I, like so many others, lost that nightly blessing habit about the same time I quit calling my mother "Mommy." It again became a daily ritual when my own children were small, and more haphazard as they "outgrew" it.

ASKING BLESSING 101

Asking blessing for others is always important, but especially in these days that are marked by so much distance and danger. At the moment we are physically distant from so many we care about, sometimes even if they live down the street from us. We are not even allowed to visit loved ones in the hospital to be with them in their suffering. And we have so little control over the economic, emotional and physical factors that surround us all.

But we can pray. We can pray for peace and safety for those we love and those we are grateful for. We can ask blessing on those who are suffering loss, danger, fear. Asking blessing can seem futile in the face of a global pandemic and economic and political struggle, and it is certainly no guarantee of physical survival. But we ask anyway.

Our asking is a moment of trust, of remembering and reasserting our belief in a loving God. When we ask blessing in the midst of tragedy we expand our view beyond the moment to the larger trajectory of eternity.

As we ask we are reminded of what binds us together, of what the Apostles' Creed calls the communion of saints. We remember the connection we have with one another in this world and the next. When we name others in blessing we are reminded to consider whether there is something we are called to do for them. We remember their goodness and how precious they are to us.

WHEN BLESSING IS FRANTIC

When my son was seven years old he developed a seizure disorder. His seizures affected the sensory part of his brain, causing him to hear and see things that weren't there. When our family doctor suggested schizophrenia as a possible diagnosis I was horrified. My prayer for Dan careened between trying to grab God by the lapels, screaming for help, and desperately trying to find the trust to more calmly put my son's welfare in God's hands. After a few agonizing months Dan was correctly diagnosed, given appropriate medication and gradually outgrew his condition, but I have never forgotten the terror and helplessness of that time.

I think God is big enough to manage our attempts to shake a blessing out of Him, and certainly many of the psalms have a frantic and even angry tone. I also know that a more calm, humble approach, when I can manage it, gives me perspective and helps me cope. A regular habit of focused prayer, and learning how to directly calm my physical reactions can help me move in that direction.

We have so little control over the economic, emotional and physical factors that surround us all.

ASKING BLESSING 901

Asking blessing for those we love isn't terribly hard, but Jesus didn't stop there. He told us also to pray for our enemies and bless those who curse us. Now *that* is a tall order. Asking blessing on those who have harmed us is tough.

On the border between St. Paul and Minneapolis is a distinctive water tower nicknamed the Witch's Cap. I travel the highway linking the cities often and for the last twenty years, whenever I pass that spot, I ask a blessing on specific people in my life who are difficult. As I round the bend and catch sight of the tower I often brace myself, because a big part of me doesn't want to be generous. But I've promised, and Jesus was serious.

We need to not only discipline ourselves to begin the prayer, but also to mind *how* we pray. Praying that someone will see the light, or do things our way, or get what's coming to them isn't asking blessing. So often when we think we're praying we're just giving God advice, much of it faulty.

Asking blessing on those who create harm is simply that–asking blessing. We ask God to bless them. We ask in a respectful tone of voice. And then we quit talking. We may stay with the request for a while, but we stop the commentary. Or at least we try to redirect our attention when our old thought loop shows up.

RESEARCH ON RESILIENCE

To my knowledge the beneficial impact of this kind of prayer on the pray-er has not been studied, but a similar secular practice—lovingkindness meditation—has mountains of articles attesting to its positive impact. Major universities across the country have studied it extensively, and their results are readily available online.

Lovingkindness meditation has a clear four-step format that invites us to consciously move from easy to hard blessing. First we activate compassion in our brains, and then we consciously expand our circle. Using the protocol, we:

1) Ask blessing for ourselves, then
2) Repeat the positive intention for someone we love, then
3) Ask blessing for someone who is neutral—perhaps a familiar face at the grocery store checkout lane.

These three blessing moments prime our hearts and our brains for the next, very hard step. Because finally—deep breath—we:

4) Ask the same blessing for someone who has harmed us or others. This can be someone we know personally, a political figure, a stranger who harmed someone we love, etc.

Research clearly demonstrates that people who regularly engage in this kind of meditation feel more compassion and behave more altruistically. In addition to research participants' reports of their experiences, these results are confirmed in brain scans and interviews with those close to them.

MOVING FORWARD

This is an especially good time to begin or strengthen a regular habit of asking blessing. Remembering to bless those we care about can be transformative. It can lessen our tendency to worry and help us resist getting distracted from important relationships.

In our current contentious climate, asking blessing on dangerous people can be a step toward healing not just ourselves but also our world. We can ask blessing on people while still holding them accountable. We can ask blessing as an alternative to the stories we tell ourselves about people who disagree with us. Imagine if everyone truly asked a blessing before every difficult negotiation, every decision that impacted others, every conversation about how to best move forward in our private and public lives.

Asking blessing on our enemies is hard. It is not for the faint-hearted.

Or perhaps, with God's help, it is.

ACTION PLAN

1) I will ask blessing on people I care about _____ times this week.   The individual(s) I will focus on include (ex: family, prayer list, friends, etc.)

2) I will ask blessing on a person or group that is difficult for me. I commit myself to not offering God advice and to call myself back from the stories I'm tempted to tell myself about them.

The Spiritual Resilience Handbook

Chapter 5: Spiritual Emotions

T hink for a minute of a few people you consider spiritually resilient. They might be famous - like Martin Luther King, Jr. or Mother Theresa - or they may include members of your own family.

Why do their faces come to mind? How would you describe them, and what qualities do they hold in common? What is it about these people that you instinctively admire and respect?

Regardless of who you chose, I would be willing to bet your examples possess a calm strength, a sense of hope and generosity, and a willingness to engage in but not get bogged down by their own and others' suffering.

Most likely they exhibit a higher than average tendency toward:

- gratitude
- hope
- compassion
- awe
- serenity
- joy
- inspiration
- love

These spiritual qualities call us–emotionally, not just intellectually–beyond our own small egos to connect with other people, creation, and God. In doing so, they allow us to experience our deepest and best selves, the part of us that is most capable of seeing reality and acting as God intends.

POSITIVE EFFECTS OF SPIRITUAL EMOTIONS

In the last few decades, members of the positive psychology movement have conducted extensive research on these and other positive emotions. Noted expert Dr. Barbara Fredrickson has documented that when we experience these emotions we are more likely to:

- think more creatively
- gain a clearer sense of perspective
- be more altruistic
- be more flexible
- be more physically healthy
- be more emotionally resilient
- make more positive choices

- experience lower levels of depression and anxiety
- be able to share these emotions effortlessly with others

Seriously, if someone announced they'd just developed a pill that would deliver these benefits, I'd be the first to sign up. Our six spiritual practices are even better. They don't cost money, don't have negative side effects, and are way more enjoyable than swallowing a pill will ever be.

Spiritual resilience is not the same as a chipper outlook. Spiritually resilient people do not live in denial about complexity or pain, and they do not put undue emphasis on their own happiness. But while spiritual resilience is not just about being happy, it is characterized by emotions that feel good. Our opening lesson focused on the practice and emotion of gratitude. Today we'll take a look at love and joy.

SPIRITUAL EMOTION: LOVE

Love can be an emotion or it can be a choice. As an emotion love is a warm, joyful, momentary connection with another. We can legitimately love nature or music or our dog or our goofy neighbor or our president. Love in the moment is spontaneous, but we often have to till our soul's soil so those spontaneous moments can happen more readily and frequently.

I've heard meditation described as a long, loving look at reality. I understand the concept, although I can't actually manage to do it all that well. I've also heard it described

34

as a time when, "I look at God and God looks at me." When we take the time to consciously place ourselves in God's presence we step into a deeper dimension of love. We increase our own capacity to give and receive, to notice and embrace love when it pops up unexpectedly.

Jesus called us to *do* love and to *experience* love. If it's true that God is love, then love does literally make the world go 'round. We need to draw on all the means at our disposal to step *on* to that merry-go-round.

SPIRITUAL EMOTION: JOY

Joy is like happiness only different. Joy runs deeper, and like hope it can exist *in spite of* rather than because of our current circumstances. People who are terminally ill can be joyful even though they are not happy about facing the end of their days on earth. Little children and puppies seem wired for joy, delighted at a leaf dancing across their path even in the most dismal surroundings.

Harvard's Dr. George Vaillant, a pioneer in studying spiritual emotions, reminds us that happiness arrives more surely as a byproduct than an object of our actions. When we try to make ourselves happy we often just make ourselves tired. When we remember to be grateful, to forgive, to pay attention to the hearts of the quirky people around us, we can be, as C.S. Lewis titled his autobiography, *Surprised By Joy*.

Joy seems to coincide with an ability to be present to the moment as it truly is. Brother David Steindl-Rast said his life in Germany during World War II was filled with great joy because he and his comrades knew death could come at any time and they therefore lived in the moment. He says,

> *Joy is something other than pleasure.*
> *Joy is the feeling of being in sync with life,*
> *in tune with the Mystery.*
> *One may have all the pleasure in the world*
> *and yet feel out of tune with life;*
> *but one may, by contrast, be screaming in anguish*
> *and yet hear deep inside the music of joy,*
> *a counterpoint bass line as it were.*

One caveat: Impressive people can be inspiring but also a little intimidating. Please don't let all this talk about spiritually resilient people leave you feeling inadequate. I'm inspired by Brother David's example, but I am confident his joyfulness is beyond me. We're not responsible for *being* Brother David for the simple reason we *are not* Brother David. Instead we are called to be moving, however slowly, toward the full expression of God's specific vision for us. And that is enough.

Quote taken from *I Am Through You So I,* David Steindl-Rast, OSB, p. 10

Recommended books:
Love 2.0, Barbara Fredrickson
Spiritual Evolution, George Vaillant

ACTION PLAN

Use this week to deepen one or more of the practices we've discussed so far.

The practice(s) I will focus on this week:

I commit to engage in them _____ times this week.

Notice if and when those practices are accompanied by an increase in love or joy. Which ones show up for you?

As you look at the list of spiritual emotions, are there a few that are characteristic of you currently? If so, which?

Are there a few in particular you would like to see more of? Can any of the practices we've discussed help?

The Power of Music

Chapter 6: The Power of Music

One day social worker Dan Cohen was reflecting on the isolation experienced by so many assisted-care facility residents, particularly those living with dementia. He thought, "If I ever find myself in that situation I hope I can still listen to the music I love." Inspired by that insight, Cohen began volunteering in a facility near his home, interviewing patients about music from their past and loading their favorite songs on iPods. Some residents who had been nonverbal for years suddenly came alive, sharing stories, rediscovering joy and literally remembering who they were. Cohen's work grew, eventually chronicled in the Sundance Audience Award-winning documentary, *Alive Inside*.

We've all had the experience of an unexpected piece of music carrying us back in time and space to a long-forgotten moment. Suddenly we're there, "seeing" faces and places we haven't thought of in years. We know experientially, and research confirms, that music can swiftly bypass the more logical and verbal parts of our brains to directly evoke moments, memories, and emotions.

Many of those memories and emotions have healing power. When Minneapolis-based musician Mark Mallman's mother died tragically, he was thrown into a series of disabling panic attacks. He assembled a "Happiness Playlist" of 100 songs, determined to listen only to joyful music until he had recovered enough to cope with his loss. When the playlist actually worked, he wrote a book by that name to help others find the same relief. (You can also find his Happiness Playlist on Spotify.)

While some of Mallman's music choices puzzle me, his book confirmed an intuition I was already exploring: We can deliberately use music to help us heal and become more spiritually resilient. This fact is no surprise to the thousands of dedicated, professionally trained music therapists in our midst.

Until the last century humans didn't have many musical choices. They were limited to their region's music, composed and performed by their neighbors and the ancestors who preceded them. Their shared regional music united and identified them; generations made, heard and danced to music together. The community owned its music.

Today we have ready access to a dizzying array of musical styles, which is wonderful. But that same diversity can contribute to our tendency to divide ourselves into musical silos according to age, class, geography and even politics. Few of us sing or play instruments together outside of church, deferring music-making to the professionals. We find persistent tension between "sacred" and "secular" music, with many a congregation split over the choice of music to be used during services. Some compromise by dividing services—and the congregation—into contemporary and traditional camps, while others see people leave altogether when a new music director sets up shop.

Since we're working on our own individual spiritual music practice, we don't have to worry about what other people think is appropriate. Whichever music will increase our experience of gratitude, hope, compassion, awe, serenity, joy, inspiration and love is exactly the music we need. "Our" music can belong to any genre and come with or without religious language. Many of us older folks will resonate most deeply with the music that touched us in our youth. What matters is that we find the right music for us, figure out how to make it available, and use it.

I have a couple of Spotify playlists, one titled Sacred, the other Healing. I continue to edit and prune each list. When I begin my morning prayer/meditation, I choose a song, listen, and then set a timer for my quiet time. The music helps me transition to a more quiet, reflective state.

ASSEMBLING AND USING YOUR OWN MUSICAL TREASURY

Your actual strategy for music as a spiritual practice will depend on how you normally access music. Here are some options:

1) Make a list of songs and sing them to yourself. It's an old and venerable tradition.

2) Play your favorite music on an instrument.

3) Assemble a stack of LP's or CD's and note which individual pieces you like best. Play them regularly.

4) Create a playlist or station on iTunes, Spotify, Pandora, or another service. Use it regularly.

5) Check the list of spiritual emotions above and see if you can find one or more pieces of music that evoke an emotion on the list. Pay special attention to those emotions you experience less frequently.

6) Talk about your playlist with someone else who is also assembling a sacred music treasury. Share stories and memories of why this music is special for you.

7) Help someone who is vulnerable create and access a playlist tailored especially for them.

Happy listening!

Whichever music will increase our experience of gratitude, hope, compassion, awe, serenity, joy, inspiration and love - that is our sacred music.

ACTION PLAN

I commit myself to spend _____ *hours this week making up a playlist of music that is sacred for me.*

I choose _____ *strategy for gathering and playing music.*

What I need in order to make this happen (online subscription, extension cord, etc.)

In the future, I would like to listen to my playlist for

___(time)___ *- per week.*

This is more likely to happen if I:

I will share this process with _____.

Taking Stock

I do not understand what I do.
For what I want to do I do not do...
I have the desire to do what is good,
but cannot carry it out.
For I do not do the good I want to do,
but the evil I do not want to do--this I keep on doing.
Romans 7:15, 18b-19

Chapter 7: Brain 101

W e've all had the experience of saying or doing something and immediately regretting it.

"How could I have done that??!!" we wonder.

For hundreds of years philosophers theorized that our intellect and will constituted our "higher selves," which had the unenviable assignment of wrestling our emotions into submission. We were encouraged to energetically scold ourselves, "Straighten up!" "Stop feeling that way!" "Get your act together.!"

Which unfortunately doesn't work very well. Those messy moments we all experience aren't simply failures in character, although character certainly has something to do with it. Our brains aren't designed to respond perfectly to vigorous self-talk, at least not when we're emotionally upset. The more we understand how our brains *do* work, the more effectively we can steer ourselves toward greater peace and better behavior.

Neuroscientist Paul MacLean suggests the brain is divided into three basic parts. The theory described below is an oversimplification, but it holds enough truth to be useful in understanding ourselves:

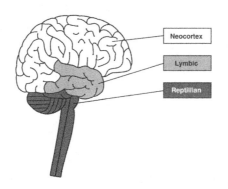

1) The most primitive part of the brain governs basic functions like breathing and our sense of balance and physical location in the world. It is sometimes called the "reptilian brain" because lizards and snakes share the same capacities.

2) The second, or limbic, section of the brain holds all the abilities we share with dogs, dolphins and elephants. It includes more sophisticated problem solving and a wider range of emotions, including our attachment to others.

3) The outermost layer of the brain, the cerebral cortex, is most highly developed in human beings. It is the site of our analytical thinking and holds capacities like language and impulse control.

So what? Why bother learning about this? It turns out the interaction among these three brain parts is one cause of our many human missteps. The reptilian/emotional brain is designed to override our thinking brain in an emergency. If someone grabs you from behind on a dark street or your toddler suddenly starts to gag, you don't have time to logically examine all your alternatives. It doesn't matter what your attacker looks like or what precisely is giving your little one trouble. You need to take action. This aspect of brain function can work for us when we're under immediate physical threat but against us in a disagreement with an employer or a loved one.

Under certain circumstances, like traumatic experiences, the communication between our thinking brain and our emotional brain can break down for an extended period of time. Telling ourselves to not be mad, to be grateful, to put things in logical perspective just doesn't get us very far. Turns out what *does* help is action that targets the emotional part of our brains directly.

Spiritual practices, for example. When we fully engage in spiritual practices, we fire up the emotional brain in line with our most deeply held beliefs and convictions. Over time we can literally reshape our brains.

Really. The change shows up on brain scans.

When our brains are activated they form something called "neural pathways." To see how they work, think of someone who annoys you. What happens when you call that person to mind? Do you find yourself reviewing the exact same grievances you've visited so many times before? Using the same language in your head? Language that maybe even embarrasses you? That's an example of a neural pathway in action.

When we engage in spiritual practices we are deliberately forming new neural pathways. It's easier for us to redirect emotional energy to an alternate neural pathway than it is to simply turn off the energy. When you write someone a note of gratitude, or ask blessing on someone you find difficult, you are laying down a tiny "groove" in your brain, similar to rainwater carving out little gullies in a hillside. If you regularly listen to music that uplifts you, you have created alternate, more positive pathways in your brain. Catching yourself ruminating and redirecting yourself to recalling a piece of music or being thankful is a neurological as well as a spiritual practice.

So do we just give up on urging ourselves to be more hopeful, compassionate, joyful or grateful? Obviously not. Instead, we can also use the logical part of our brains to remind ourselves to tap into spiritual practices that touch our emotions directly. The result is an expanded capacity to listen to our own best selves–and the promptings of the Spirit.

When we engage in spiritual practices
we are deliberately forming new neural pathways.

Taking Stock

Chapter 8: Taking Stock

B y now you may be feeling a bit overwhelmed. Chances are you picked up this book because you or someone you care about is feeling distress. You were interested because the destination–spiritual resilience– struck a chord. At this point it may seem like you've simply added more responsibilities that you're expected to haul around. In this chapter we're going to take a little time to pull out the road map, see where we've been and where we're headed, and check on how the path is working for you.

We'll start by reviewing the key landmarks framing our adventure. For this trek, we've agreed:

1) Spiritual resilience is the ability to maintain a sturdy positive spirit and a clear sense of purpose and meaning even in the face of suffering. There are three elements in this definition: positive spirit, purpose and meaning, and

suffering. Our work is focused primarily on methods for strengthening a positive spirit.

2) We've said a positive spirit is marked by eight spiritual emotions: gratitude, hope, compassion, awe, serenity, joy, inspiration and love. Our goal in this series is to deepen our experience of these emotions and support others in seeking the same.

3) We are using six spiritual practices in our quest: gratitude, blessing, surrender/letting go, service, music, and one-liners.

4) We are including the mind/body/spirit connection by examining and using basic neuroscience and research from the positive psychology movement.

This is a tall order for a small book. My hope is that when you're done reading you will have enough comfort with, and understanding of, these practices that you'll be able to naturally weave *moments* of them throughout your day.

In addition, you may regularly set aside ten to twenty minutes for focused effort, or you may not. Regular focused time is really, really helpful, but it's just not going to happen for everyone. Even if you "only" pull out a practice when you catch yourself heading down an anxiety, grief or anger rabbit hole, that will make a difference.

LIKE FREE THROWS FOR THE HEART

This book is a little like basketball camp. If you sign up for basketball camp you expect to spend a fair amount of time practicing drills and free throws. Without practice, few of us would be able to hit the backboard, let alone get that ball to swish through the net. Drills may seem artificial, but the habits they cultivate prepare players to up their game when fans are in the stands and the opposing team is making life difficult.

This "spiritual resilience camp" is a time to learn and deepen six spiritual practices so we can find them when we need them. So far we've covered gratitude, blessing, and music. In the next few weeks we'll practice surrender/letting go, loving service, and one-liners. You may already have established a good rhythm in your life for some habits; others may need more deliberate attention. My hope is that by the end of this book you will have engaged in each practice to the point where it feels natural. You'll walk away equipped to pick and choose, drawing on them in whatever way best suits you.

For example, I have a fairly-regular-but-not-perfect twenty-minute morning practice, focused primarily on letting go and asking blessing. I'm pretty good at spontaneous moments of gratitude throughout the day, although I can lapse into brattiness between thank-you's. I listen to my Spotify playlists in spurts, and wish I was more consistent because I notice the difference. I'm on furlough as a volunteer tutor, but hope to get back into action soon.

Worry and wanting to control are my personal weaknesses. My daughter is a social worker in a shelter, dealing face-to-face with people experiencing homelessness and mental health issues. Her husband is an ER nurse in a designated COVID-response hospital. I am scared to death about their exposure to the coronavirus. When I begin to mentally chase what-ifs, I call on a spiritual practice. I try to switch to thanking God for them, for moments we've laughed together, for their beautiful spirits. Or I ask blessing on them, their colleagues, the people they serve. Or I put on a piece of music that somehow captures sadness and hope at the same time. Or I silently repeat "Blessed are you, O Lord our God, creator of the universe." Or I sew a few face masks. Or...

You know your own life, your time commitments, your level of distress. You know which practices already come naturally to you and which might offer a good stretch. There's no such thing as perfect spiritual practice (at least not in this life), just as there's no such thing as a perfect basketball game.

But we're getting out there. And that matters.

This course is like
free throw practice for the heart.

ACTION PLAN

Take a few minutes to take stock of where you are right now. So far we have covered:
- Using gratitude practices
- Becoming more aware of our bodies
- Asking blessing - when it's easy and when it's hard
- The benefits of positive spiritual emotions
- The power of music
- Understanding the brain

Which of these lessons have I actually used?

Have I experienced any benefits? If so, what?

Which would I like to use more? What is my commitment there?

Letting Go

Chapter 9: Letting Go

Lord, thank you for the gift of this day.
Please give me the grace
to live it according to your will.

The fundamental goal of this program is to consciously connect with God and allow ourselves to be transformed into the persons we were created to be. This new person isn't a sanitized, more compliant version of our current selves, but rather a unique, loving, courageous, and joyful manifestation of God's abundant vision for us. We will never perfectly realize this vision here on earth, but we can choose to move toward it.

WE NEED HELP

If we could get there on our own we would probably be there by now. Unfortunately, our shortcomings stubbornly persist in spite of our best efforts. Take a minute to review your week–or maybe just your morning. Can you name any moments when you were less courageous, kind or generous than you would have liked? Me too. (If you can't recall any moments of weakness, we need a whole different conversation.)

In order to let God help us we need to be willing to let go of our habitual way of doing things. So often we act like a child running to her parents with a broken toy, frantically begging them to fix it. Until she's willing to let go of the toy, to put it into their hands and let them work on it, the toy and her distress cannot be mended. In order for things to change, we have to admit the chances that we are right and God is wrong are pretty darn slim. We must let go of our attempts to control; we need to get out of the way and let God go to work.

WHAT SURRENDER IS NOT -
AND WHAT TRUE SURRENDER LOOKS LIKE

Many people stall out on letting go because they misunderstand the concept. Surrender is not about becoming a doormat. "Let go and let God" is a great slogan, but only when properly understood. The famous Serenity Prayer says, "God, grant me the serenity to accept the things I cannot change, the courage to change the things I can, and the wisdom to know the difference." True surrender helps us discern more accurately when to let go and when to stand up and be counted.

Surrendering to God is not about giving up our free will but about using our freedom differently. Letting go doesn't ask us to be passive; it encourages us to be coachable. A coachable athlete doesn't lose his individuality, talents or skills. A good coach doesn't take the ball and play the game for her athletes. In an ideal coach/athlete relationship the coach offers knowledge and inspiration that the athlete incorporates into his performance. A talented athlete who resists wise coaching is likely to miss his full potential. We find the freedom in this paradox only by living it.

To try another analogy, surrender is like putting a canoe into the water and allowing the current to carry us. We still steer, we still need to watch out for boulders and navigate through rapids, but we quit trying to paddle upstream and we let the current carry us when it can. Beats the heck out of trying to drag that canoe overland ourselves.

Surrender does not need to be about admitting defeat, although too often we choose to let go only when all else has failed. God honors our intention, even when we surrender reluctantly. When we let go, however imperfectly we get there, we make our broken lives accessible to God's loving hands.

LIKE A BUNCH OF ROCKS

A long time ago a friend suggested an exercise she used when she was having trouble letting go. Her suggestion stayed with me and I have used it countless times over the years.

Call to mind a person or situation that is not as you would like. Take a minute to really focus on your dilemma–not analyzing it, just focusing your attention. Now visualize the person(s) or situation(s) as stones. Take a minute to imagine as many rocks as you need to set the stage.

Next, imagine yourself placing each of your stones on the ground in front of you. Imagine God's love and light warming and illuminating them. Take a moment to notice if anything looks different.

Now put your hands behind your back.

Most of us flash a knowing smile at the thought of putting our hands behind our backs. We have a tendency to kid ourselves into thinking we've let go when we haven't, and the image catches us out. When you truly let go, even for a few seconds, you'll feel a kind of physical release.

You may grab on to the issue again 30 seconds or four days later. That's to be expected. The best response is to just let go again.

And again.

And again.

THE LIMITS OF EFFORT

Our capacity to let go is limited by many things: our history, our intention, our body's inherited biochemistry, our brains' response to stress and trauma. During an especially difficult time in my life I felt as though I was trying to let go every two minutes and could see absolutely no improvement in my emotional state or my behavioral capacity. I felt as if I were paddling mightily and staying in exactly the same spot on the stream, the sound of the rapids around the curve pounding in my ears. I believed then, and believe now, that without these practices I would have been swept further downstream, but I sure wasn't finding much respite in the moment even with sustained effort. Spiritual practices are useful tools in the challenging and complex undertaking that is life, but they are only tools. They can't fix everything.

SO WHAT, THEN?

Like an athlete listening for a coach's voice, we try to hear, pay attention and then behave accordingly. Sometimes we hear a message and decide to ignore it. Sometimes we notice a shift in ourselves or our perspective, and sometimes we don't. Learning to let go, to allow ourselves to be coached, takes time and practice.

As St. Paul said, we now see only through a glass, darkly. (1 Cor. 13:12) Our spiritual practices help us rub our sleeves on the glass, clearing a space we can peer through, catching glimpses of the amazing picture on the other side.

So let's begin.

ACTION PLAN

1) Is there someone who could coach me in this process? If so, who? Am I willing to ask for coaching?

2) What resistances do I encounter against letting go? Name them and try to let go of them.

3) Am I willing to select an issue and try turning it over to God? If so, what?

4) How/when am I willing to focus on letting go? How many times per week am I willing to commit to consciously letting go?

Remember to watch for a shift in awareness or outcomes after letting go. Sometimes they happen and sometimes they don't, but if we don't remember to pay attention we can miss a lot.

God, grant me
the serenity to accept the things I cannot change,
the courage to change the things I can,
and the wisdom to know the difference.

Chapter 10: Serenity, Awe & the Body's Feedback Loop

I f we're honest, one reason we're drawn to seek spiritual resilience is that we want to feel better. Whether we're coping with relationship issues, financial stress, loss of a loved one or the uncertainty brought on by a pandemic, we would like to be able to reduce the wear and tear on our emotions. Spiritual resilience includes the ability to enjoy life at a higher level and to waste less time spinning our wheels. It also offers more.

In previous chapters we looked at the deeper dimensions of gratitude, hope and joy. We distinguished between gratitude and appreciation; between joy and happiness. We said spiritual emotions were not simply an escape from pain but rather resulted from our ability to transcend pain by tapping into an underlying sacred connection.

Today we'll spend some time considering the spiritual emotions of serenity and awe. At the end of the chapter we'll look at the body's information feedback system and the impact it has on our emotional state.

SPIRITUAL EMOTION: SERENITY

While spiritual serenity calms our innate fight-or-flight response, it is not to be confused with a numbed-out, frozen emotional state or with being asleep.

Serenity is an indication that we are at peace with ourselves and our world. It arises not from a lack of caring but rather from a deep acceptance of what is and the ability to see life in perspective.

Different faith traditions offer varying foundations for serenity. Buddhist serenity rests on the insight that everything changes and our attachments and attempts to be in control are futile. A Christian's serenity is rooted in Jesus' example and ultimate triumph over suffering and death. The word *Islam* translates as *the serenity that comes from surrendering to God,* while Jewish serenity trusts in God's covenant even in the face of persistent persecution and tragedy. People in Twelve Step recovery programs rely on surrender to a Higher Power as the turning point in finding and maintaining their sobriety.

Serenity is a peace that transcends current circumstances and rests in the very deepest recesses of our hearts. Brother David Steindl-Rast says, "Going forward in faith is not a train ride; it's more like walking on water. The life of faith is a continual test of trust."

Peter was able to walk on water until his trust wavered. Serenity lies in being able to keep our eyes on the prize, finding the calm center of the storm even when the wind and waves are churning around us.

SPIRITUAL EMOTION: AWE

Awe stops us in our tracks when we come upon a sunset, a night sky sprinkled with stars, or a large body of water. Awe immediately makes us aware of scale: our tiny presence in the face of immensity. When we look at a night sky we usually feel small in a good way (unless we're feeling particularly lonely or confused, when the view can either heal us or make us feel a whole lot worse.)

When we encounter the truly awesome, we are reminded that we are not the masters of the universe, and that we and the universe are better off for that fact. We have a sense of being part of something greater than ourselves, something completely outside our control. Awe transcends logic and is beyond argument; it is a way of directly knowing.

Until fairly recently most humans lived in close contact with nature. While the experience wasn't always pleasant, it had a certain humbling effect. The limits of human control were hard to escape, even for the very wealthy. C.S. Lewis once said that humility is not denying our talents but instead remembering they are gift. Awe evaporates rather than crushes the arrogance that leads us to believe we are the center of the universe and the source of its benefits.

To keep our egos in check, to keep our sense of the world reasonably accurate, we need to revisit awe frequently. We experience awe when we give our attention to something marvelous, whether to the elegance of a mathematical equation, the majesty of a piece of music or the precision of a colony of ants whisking their eggs to safety after their hill has been totaled by a toddler with a stick. If we pay attention, opportunities for awe are everywhere.

THE BODY'S INFORMATION LOOP

Here we're going to rather abruptly shift gears and revisit our study of how our nervous systems play a part in moving us toward spiritual emotions. We've discussed the three-part brain and how our brains form neural pathways that impact our thinking Some describe this phenomenon as, "Neurons that fire together, wire together."

Today we're going to build on that awareness and examine the feedback loop that runs from your brain to the rest of your body and back.

We used to believe our bodies took information in through our senses, our brains processed it, and then directed our bodies to take action. We now know that the nervous system embedded in every inch of our bodies sends information to our brains in an ongoing feedback loop, often intensifying our reactions to an event. Way too often, this loop gets in our way.

For example:
- Event: I say hello to a coworker who seems to deliberately ignore me.
- Brain's interpretation: I assume the coworker is mad at me—or stuck up.
- Physical reaction: My blood pressure goes up, my muscles tighten, my stomach starts to hurt.
- Feedback loop: My brain recognizes the physical reactions in my body and gets alarmed. My brain assumes the physical reaction is a response to a real threat. It then starts checking my environment for problems, and is unfortunately expert at finding them even if they're not there. I ramp up my story about my snotty coworker and start to remember unpleasant episodes with other coworkers that I'd forgotten. Things go downhill from there.

Our spiritual practices can help us interrupt a negative feedback cycle. I leave work, notice the sun setting, and thank God for the beauty. My physical reaction, which has been simmering and perhaps prompting me to take action that makes things worse, settles down. The positive effect spills over into the rest of my day.

If I pay attention, I can learn from this moment to:

1) Not assume that just because I'm agitated there is therefore something terribly wrong, and,

2) Realize if I take action to calm my physical agitation I can settle into a clearer sense of reality and improve my response.

This week, use body awareness to notice a moment when your physical reaction is causing you to blow an event out of proportion. Try using a spiritual practice you've learned to directly intervene with your physical response.

Quote from *I Am Through You So I*, p. 77

Serenity, Awe...

ACTION PLAN

The task in this lesson is to become more aware of the negative feedback circle when it happens in our lives.

On a scale of 1/10, which do I tend to lean toward?

Anger/resentment   *Sadness/depression*

Fear/worry   *Fighting to control*

This week, notice when you start getting caught up into one of these cycles.
1) Notice what your body is feeling.
2) Notice the story you're telling yourself.
3) Try using a spiritual practice to shift your thinking and your heart
4) Notice if your body feels different after using the spiritual practice.

Chapter 11: Compassion and Inspiration

O n August 23, 1989, nearly two million people formed a human chain spanning 419 miles across the small Eastern European countries of Latvia, Estonia and Lithuania. The event was part of a larger struggle challenging the Soviet Union's domination of the Baltic region. Protestors kept their spirits up by singing, drawing on the region's long history of massive choral music events celebrating Baltic culture and history. The effort sustained them in their ultimately successful struggle for freedom. It continues even today to inspire people across the globe in the documentary *The Singing Revolution.*

INSPIRATION

Inspiration is a friendlier name for an emotion psychologists call *moral elevation,* which is our response when we witness an act of moral beauty. When we feel inspired our hearts are touched, the world lights up, and we feel a spontaneous desire to be and do better. In the case of the Singing Revolution, we see an enormous crowd of vulnerable people standing up to a brutal regime. In addition to being incredibly brave, they also created a magical, astonishingly beautiful moment. When we view a picture or listen to a recording of them singing we respond both to their courage and to the majesty of their music. We are moved to think that had we been there we might even have taken part in the moment.

True stories of heroism are inspiring, and they are all around us. These stories don't always have to be real. Our hunger for inspiration accounts in part for the incredible success of the Star Wars and Harry Potter series. Music, art, dance and theater at their best all have the power to evoke an intense sense of the greater possibilities in ourselves and others. For a striking example, check out Playing for Change, which for years has gathered musicians from around the world to create music videos that immediately put us in touch with hope and the universal resilience of the human spirit.

A powerful moment of inspiration can stop us in our tracks, pick us up and set us down facing in an entirely new direction. Spiritual heroes often describe a watershed moment in their lives when they were overcome by an inspiration that triggered a long and sometimes painful process of moral transformation. Many of us can look back on people or moments that were turning points, inspiring us to aim higher, try harder, see more in ourselves and the world. The feeling of inspiration is particularly important in our cynical age, when so many we have looked up to turn out to have feet made of clay and sometimes knives in their back pockets.

COMPASSION

We've all grown accustomed to Youtube moments going viral. Some explode onto the scene because they're funny, others because they're controversial. Some of the best hit a nerve because they inspire us to compassion.

One such moment is an encounter between Pope Francis and a little boy who is frightened that his beloved deceased father, an atheist, will be unable to go to heaven. The little boy's grief, and Pope Francis' sensitivity and compassion, touch our hearts and make as all want to be a little better. To see the moment captured on video, google "Pope Francis little boy."

Compassion lies at the core of every great spiritual tradition. It is a feeling of care and concern for others, especially for those who are suffering. Compassion is distinct from pity and empathy. Pity is often criticized as patronizing, springing essentially from a one-up position. Most of us resist being the object of others' pity. Empathy involves feeling another's pain as if it were our own, and brain imaging technology shows the pain centers of empathetic individuals' brains light up when they observe other's suffering.

Compassion goes a step beyond empathy to include an impulse to take action to help. Compassion includes an element of discomfort that prompts us to do something to relieve other's difficulty. It is at the heart of every great heroic story and every great spiritual tradition. When we witness compassion we are inspired to be braver and more generous ourselves.

Compassion and inspiration are good for our souls. Like the other spiritual emotions we've looked at, they help us thrive and take action to help others prosper as well. Under their influence, we are invited to see beyond the immediate to the possible, and to begin to live into that possibility. Today and every day.

Compassion and Inspiration

ACTION PLAN

1) Make a list of heroes and saints who inspire you.

2) Watch a movie or video clip that inspires you.

3) Read an account of the life of a saint or hero.

4) Share some of those resources with another person.

Chapter 12: One-liners

"It is what it is."

We've all heard the phrase.
No one knows who first said it.
No one ever explains it.
Surprisingly, for some reason it often seems to settle us down without much debate.

QUICK RESET

One-liners can do that. When we hear the term *one-liner* we often think of a quick joke, but in this context we mean a simple phrase that helps us shift our current perception to one that is more helpful. The psychological term for this process is *positive cognitive reframe.*

One-liners

We all use one-liners throughout the day, saying some out loud and repeating others silently to ourselves. We may have been handed our stash growing up or gathered them over the years. You probably have a few favorites without being fully conscious of them.

Political movements and product champions know the power of a good catchphrase. In the world of today's social media, a one-liner can ignite a crowd and develop a life of its own almost instantly. One-liners can be powerful forces for good–or for destruction.

Some, like *No pain no gain* and Nike's *Just Do It,* grow out of a particular culture. Some seem to just float around everywhere. You may use some of your grandmother's favorites. We resonate with some of the catchphrases we hear and instinctively reject others. Becoming conscious of our collection, weeding out those that are unhelpful and consciously adding others, can be a powerful way of correcting our course throughout the day.

Here are a few positive examples:

Keep on keeping on.
Do the next right thing.
One day at a time.
Progress, not perfection.
If nothing changes, nothing changes.
First things first.
Hallelujah anyway.
What went right today?

One-liners show up on calendars, t-shirts and framed on walls. Years ago I visited a parish office that had *John 1:20* displayed on a plaque. The reference reminded staff and visitors, "I am not the Messiah." From time to time we all need that reality check.

WHAT THIS MIGHT LOOK LIKE

The first step is to become more aware of our current self-talk. If you make a quick inventory of aspects of your personality that could use a little help, you'll probably find one-liners at work. A small change, if it feels authentic, can make a big difference.

For example, I tend to be just a tiny bit judgmental. When people say about someone, "They're just doing the best they can with what they've got," I'm rarely convinced. But I *do* shift gears when I remind myself, "I have no idea what brings this person to this moment." That statement is absolutely true. I don't entirely know what brings *me* to this moment, so how can I know all of someone else's story or the depths of another's heart?

When someone tailgates me or cuts me off in traffic, I tell myself, "I'm so glad I don't have to go home with you." I don't think it's a framing Jesus would use, or maybe even approve of, but it helps me.

Hitting a quick reset button can save us from useless mind chatter and sometimes prevent an unwise action.

IN PRAYER AND MEDITATION

A second type of one-liner is a word or phrase that is repeated, silently or out loud, during prayer or meditation. We use this word or phrase to gently redirect ourselves when our minds scamper off, as they invariably do. *Open awareness* meditation, which is sometimes described as emptying the mind, is notoriously difficult. *Focused* meditation where we use a word or phrase to call ourselves back, while not easy, is more attainable. Simply having a focus helps us manage our scattered, random thinking and create more space to listen to the Spirit.

At some point I read that if you use a phrase repeatedly in prayer it will eventually begin to permeate your day, coming spontaneously to mind without effort. I was skeptical, confident such things happened only to holy people.

Until it began happening to me. I had tried various phrases over the course of a couple years, none of which seemed to be a fit. Eventually I settled into "Blessed are you, O Lord, our God, creator of the universe." A competent meditation teacher would say the phrase is too long and complicated, but I love its ancient history in Judaism and Christianity. For some reason I adopted it. Sure enough, as I'm sitting at a stop sign or staring at the ceiling in the middle of the night or weeding my garden or preparing for a difficult conversation the phrase floats up without my bidding it. I am always grateful for the reset.

Some examples:

Thank you.
Jesus.
Not my will but yours.
Light my path.
Be with me, Lord.
Peace.
Your grace is sufficient.

Whether a daytime slogan or a prayer-time anchor, one-liners have a subtle, and sometimes not-so-subtle, ability to move us toward spiritual resilience. Like searching for a pair of comfortable shoes, you need to try on a few and take them out on the road. After you find the right collection and break them in, you won't even be aware you're wearing them.

Until you stop and remember what those old blisters on your toes felt like.

ACTION PLAN

1) Jot down a few of the less-helpful phrases that characterize your response to an unpleasant event or situation.

2) Take a look at the list of in-the-moment positive one-liners. Are there a few that could work for you? Are you aware of some others that would be helpful? Jot them down.

3) What is a word or phrase that could be helpful when you are praying or meditating? If you don't already, try bringing the word or phrase into your prayer when you find your mind wandering. What do you notice?

Chapter 13: Loving Service

J esus didn't come just to make us feel good. In fact, he had all kinds of unsettling messages like "Take up your cross and follow me." "Feed the hungry." "Visit the imprisoned." He wasn't kidding.

Positive spiritual emotions by their very nature bring us beyond ourselves to connect with God, other creatures and our wisest selves. However, if we seek these emotions simply to benefit ourselves, they turn into something very different. When we make it all about us we transform a flowing stream into a stagnant pool.

SPIRITUAL PRACTICE: SERVICE

We don't generally think of emotions as having a purpose, but they do. Many prime us to take action. A painful sensation like fear prompts us to avoid a situation or throw up a defense, while loneliness stirs us to reach out to connect with other people.

Positive spiritual emotions like compassion and inspiration prepare us to take action to help, to make the world a better place. The emotions are bittersweet. On the one hand we are filled with a sense of the beauty of what might be, while at the same time being tugged by the undertow of sadness or even outrage at what is. We sense for a moment a world that makes sense and where everyone thrives, while at the same time having a heightened awareness of the suffering of the world as it is. We simultaneously experience deep joy and intense pain.

As I struggle to come to grips with the suffering in our world I am aware of wanting to expose myself to practices, stories, and conversations that bring me to balance. I want to be informed and aware of the terrifying reality unfolding around us, but not to the point where it paralyzes me. When my brain starts to spin into anxiety or despair, I pull out one of the spiritual practices we've discussed to help me get back to center.

But I am also aware the purpose of these practices is not to sedate me or to create a bubble protecting me from my own or others' suffering. A healthy dose of reality creates the discomfort we need to do something. The world needs us, and we need to be in contribution. Like our other spiritual practices, service also has plenty of research verifying its positive impact on our wellbeing. We are wired to connect and to care.

MAKING A DIFFERENCE

A study on soldiers fighting in World War II yielded some surprising results. The majority of soldiers who spent more than 60 days out in the field, subjected to unrelenting bombardment from above, reported eventually going numb, unable to feel anything. In contrast, fighter pilots, whose units were known to sometimes suffer a 50% mortality rate, were optimistic and enthusiastic about their work.

The difference? A sense of efficacy and control.

Part of our distress at this time is a feeling of helplessness. Like field soldiers in an extended conflict, we are at risk of losing the ability to think and to feel. Taking action gives us a sense of power, a knowledge that even though we can't fix the world we can make a difference in our corner.

One of our current losses is that our old ways of being in contribution have disappeared, at least temporarily. Many schools and social service agencies have closed or cut back; volunteers have been furloughed. For a time many of us have been like deer in headlights, frozen in place with little bandwidth available to think creatively beyond our own small circle. But the need is greater now than ever, and those of us with capacity and resources need to become creative in finding ways to be of actual practical support to others. We will benefit as deeply as they.

SPIRITUAL EMOTION: HOPE

Hope is not the same as optimism. Optimism is the expectation, realistic or not, that things are going to turn out well. Hope can exist even in situations where there is no possibility of a positive physical outcome. Hope has been described as an arm reaching out into the darkness. Hope increases our capacity to be kind and courageous; it can be a source of healing even when there is no possibility of a cure. Trust in a God who loves us, and a belief in a positive afterlife, gives us a sense of perspective that helps us see beyond the immediate.

Hopeful people keep trying even when all seems lost. They refuse to accept ultimate defeat even, sometimes, in the face of certain death. Hope bestows courage and the capacity for action; Gerald May, M.D. puts it, "Hope frees the will."

1 Cor. 13:13 says, "Faith, hope and love will last forever, but the greatest of these is love." As a kid I appreciated the importance and challenge of being faithful and loving, but I could never figure out why hope made the list. Why make such a big deal about hope? What's so hard about being hopeful? Now I get it. In the darkness of today's world, hope is harder to come by and therefore all the more precious.

ACTION PLAN

1) If you are not engaged in regular service at the moment, and if your life allows it, brainstorm some possible courses of action for you. (Remember, Jesus didn't say anything about this being convenient. We need to stretch.) In general, we're looking at the needs of those beyond our own families. You can find some ideas at https://findyourworkmn.org.

2) Jot down a plan that will help you move into action on this.
- Who do you need to talk to?
- What do you need to do to clear space in your week?
- Is there someone or some thing you can use to keep you motivated?

3) (Perhaps) Invite someone to join you in this adventure.

4) If you feel stuck, try surrendering the situation to God. Then look actively to see what shows up.

Part of our distress at this time
is a feeling of helplessness...
We need to become creative in finding ways
to be of actual practical support to others.

Chapter 14: Looking Ahead

So there you have it.

In these pages we've considered six spiritual habits that research tells us have the potential to help us navigate today's stormy waters. We've reminded ourselves of which emotions feed our spirits, and discussed how our bodies bring mischief or strength to the mind/body/spirit dimension.

You've had a chance to practice a bit, and perhaps have shared some of your experiences with others. My hope is that we not only use these practices ourselves, but also that we create mini-cultures where we speak more freely about the life of the spirit and encourage others to do the same.

I pray you've discovered some tools that can bring you greater peace, compassion and joy. Alone and together, we can create space in our lives for the moments of homecoming that remind us of who and Whose we are.

There must be always remaining in every life,
some place for the singing of angels,
some place for that which in itself
is breathless and beautiful.

Howard Thurman

Amen to that.

About the Author

Connie Fourré is an award-winning author and educator currently working in spiritual resilience education and interfaith relations. She has presented at conferences and workshops nationally and in Canada on spirituality, social justice and service learning. Her books have been translated into Spanish and Indonesian. Retired from full-time work as a high school faith formation director and wellness coordinator, she lives with her husband in the greater Minneapolis area.

For more information, see
https://spiritualresilienceproject.org.   or
https://conniefourre.com

Made in the USA
Monee, IL
16 January 2021